CULTURE IN ACTION

Gwen Stefani

Elizabeth Raum

Chicago, Illinois

www.heinemannraintree.com
Visit our website to find out
more information about
Heinemann-Raintree books.

To order:

☎ Phone 888-454-2279

💻 Visit www.heinemannraintree.com
to browse our catalog and order online.

©2010 Raintree
an imprint of Capstone Global Library, LLC
Chicago, Illinois

Edited by Louise Galpine, Abby Colich, and Laura J. Hensley
Designed by Kimberly Miracle and Betsy Wernert
Original illustrations © Capstone Global Library Ltd.
Illustrated by kja-artists.com
Picture research by Hannah Taylor
Production by Alison Parsons
Originated by Dot Gradations Ltd.
Printed and Bound in the United States
by Corporate Graphics

13 12 11 10 09
10 9 8 7 6 5 4 3 2 1

Library of Congress Cataloging-in-Publication Data

Raum, Elizabeth.
  Gwen Stefani / Elizabeth Raum.
    p. cm. -- (Culture in action)
  Includes bibliographical references and index.
  ISBN 978-1-4109-3395-9 (hc) -- ISBN 978-1-4109-3412-3
(pb)
  1. Stefani, Gwen, 1969---Juvenile literature. 2. Women
singers--United States--Biography--Juvenile literature. 3.
Women rock musicians--United States--Biography--Juvenile
literature. I. Title.
  ML3930.S74R38 2008
  782.42164092--dc22
  [B]
                        2008053048

Acknowledgments

The author and publishers are grateful to the following for
permission to reproduce copyright material: © Capstone
Publishers p. 23 (Karon Dubke); Corbis pp. 9 (Kurt Krieger),
10 (Reuters/John Hayes), 12 (Tim Mosenfelder), 18 (Reuters/
Ethan Miller), 20 (Reuters/Seth Wenig), 21 (ZUMA/Karl
Larsen), 27 top (Reuters/Mark Blinch); Getty Images
pp. 8 (Tim Mosenfelder), 13 bottom (AMA/Kevin Winter),
24 bottom (Emmanuel Faure), 25 (Fox/Frank Micelotta);
Photoshot pp. 4 (Newscom), 5 (Starstock/Gary Lee),
6 (© Starstock), 15 (Starstock/Joerg Carstensen); Redferns
pp. 16 (Harry Herd), 27 bottom (Phil Dent); Rex Features
pp. 7 (BEI/Jim Smeal), 13 top (Everett Collection/© 20th
Century Fox Film Corp All rights reserved), 14, 19
(Peter Brooker), 24 top (Steve Connolly), 26 (BEI/
Gregory Pace).

Icon and banner images supplied by Shutterstock: © Alexander
Lukin, © ornitopter, © Colorlife, and © David S. Rose.

Cover photograph of Gwen Stefani performing reproduced
with permission of Getty Images/FilmMagic/Jeff Kravitz.

We would like to thank Nancy Harris and Jackie Murphy for
their invaluable help in the preparation of this book.

Contents

Pop Music Icon 4

Early Life 6

The Road to Success 8

Sounds of Music 12

Fashion Icon. 18

Celebrity!. 24

Timeline *28*

Glossary *30*

Find Out More. *31*

Index *32*

Some words are printed in bold, **like this**. You can find out what they mean by looking in the glossary on page 30.

Pop Music Icon

Gwen Stefani is a popular singer, songwriter, and fashion designer. Fans immediately recognize her girlish voice. Even though her music moves to a quick drumbeat, Gwen's words never get lost. She sings so clearly that fans can understand all her **lyrics**.

In 2005 one of Gwen's songs was the first song in the world to sell more than one million **digital downloads**. Her CDs have sold in the millions, and she is a star around the world.

Pop singer Gwen Stefani performs in California at the beginning of her 2007 "Sweet Escape" tour.

Some of Gwen Stefani's awards

YEAR	AWARD	FOR
2001	Grammy Award	Best Female Video Award (with Eve)
2005	Brit Award	Best International Female
2005	MTV Music Video Award	Best **Choreography** (dance) Award
2008	People's Choice Award	Favorite Female Singer

Gwen is shown here in 2005 holding her Brit Award.

Style

Fans admire Gwen's style—her clothes, hairstyle, and makeup. In 1997 *People* magazine named her one of "The 50 Most Beautiful People in the World." When Gwen noticed that fans were copying her clothing, she began her own fashion line.

Gwen Stefani is recognized wherever she goes. Magazines, newspapers, and the Internet carry stories about her. But she was not always famous. Gwen began life in an ordinary family in an ordinary town. She had to work hard to become successful.

Pop idol

A person who receives a lot of attention from fans and from **media** such as newspapers and magazines is often called an **icon** or an **idol**. People have called Gwen Stefani a pop music icon as well as a fashion icon. Fans flock to her concerts and copy her style.

Early Life

Gwen Renée Stefani was born on October 3, 1969, in Anaheim, California. Her father worked for Yamaha, a Japanese motorcycle company. His stories about Japan captivated Gwen.

Gwen, her sister, Jill, and her brothers, Todd and Eric, lived at home with their parents. As a child, Gwen would pretend to be a famous singer. She liked to dress up and enjoyed watching movies, especially *The Muppet Movie*, *Annie*, and *The Sound of Music*. Gwen and her brother Eric would put on puppet shows.

Gwen enjoyed watching the movie *Annie*, which came out in 1982.

School

Gwen made friends easily. But school was difficult for her. She has **dyslexia** (see box at right), a learning disability. It makes reading, writing, and spelling very difficult.

Gwen attended Loara High School in Anaheim, California. Her friends called her Sunshine. When she joined the swim team, they began to call her Frog because she was a good swimmer.

Gwen played a small flute called the piccolo in her high school band. She liked to sing, too. In a high school talent show, she sang a song from *The Sound of Music*. While she was in high school, Gwen cleaned floors at a Dairy Queen restaurant to earn money.

Dyslexia

People with dyslexia are often highly intelligent and creative. However, they have trouble understanding written information. Even though schoolwork can be difficult, many people with dyslexia are successful. Walt Disney, the founder of Disneyland, had dyslexia. So did Thomas Edison, the inventor of the lightbulb, and Pablo Picasso, a famous painter and sculptor.

The Road to Success

When Gwen was in high school, she liked the British **ska** band Madness (see box at right). In 1986 her brother Eric and his friend John Spence formed their own ska band. It was called No Doubt. They invited 17-year-old Gwen to sing.

In December 1987 Gwen became the lead singer for No Doubt. The band played at clubs in California. Later, they toured the country.

Ska

Ska is a form of music that began in the 1950s on the island of Jamaica, in the West Indies. It combines African rhythms with Jamaican **folk music** (see page 12) and U.S. **jazz**. Jamaican **immigrants** brought the music to Great Britain and the United States.

Some members of No Doubt changed over time. This photo shows Gwen with the members of No Doubt in 1996. Pictured from left are Tony Kanal, Gwen Stefani, Tom Dumont, and Adrian Young.

In 1995 No Doubt released an album called *Tragic Kingdom*. It went on to be number one on *Billboard* magazine's "Hot 100" chart for nine weeks. No Doubt went on a worldwide tour starting in 1996.

Songwriter

Some of No Doubt's biggest hits were songs that Gwen wrote. She wrote about her feelings in songs such as "Just a Girl" and "Don't Speak" from *Tragic Kingdom*. She wrote "Marry Me" and "Simple Kind of Life" for the album *Return of Saturn*. These songs were about her hope to one day become a wife and mother.

In 2004 Gwen attended the MTV Europe Music Awards in Rome, Italy.

Big sales

ARTIST	ALBUM NAME	DATE	NUMBER OF ALBUMS SOLD (WORLDWIDE)
No Doubt	*Tragic Kingdom*	1995	15 million
No Doubt	*Return of Saturn*	2000	1.4 million
No Doubt	*Rock Steady*	2001	3 million
Gwen Stefani	*Love.Angel.Music.Baby.*	2004	6 million
Gwen Stefani	*Sweet Escape*	2006	3.5 million

Solo artist

After 17 years together, No Doubt took a break. In early 2003 Gwen began recording a solo album.

It took Gwen and other musicians more than a year to complete the album, *Love.Angel.Music.Baby.* It sold a half million copies in two weeks. In 2006 Gwen released another solo album, *Sweet Escape.*

On stage

In 2007 Gwen toured Europe, Australia, and Asia as a solo artist. Fans flocked to see her shows. A band played while Gwen sang and danced in front of large video screens and flashing lights. **Hip-hop** dancers in funky, colorful costumes shared the stage with her (see box below).

Gwen includes lively dance numbers in her shows.

Hip-hop

Hip-hop dancing was invented in New York City in the 1970s. This high-energy style includes break dancing, popping, and krumping. Dancers leap, dive, spin, and twirl. They may look like puppets on a string, using both smooth and jerky moves.

Create a dance routine

Listen to one of the following songs from Gwen's *Sweet Escape* album. Each has a strong beat:

> "Breakin' Up"
> "Wind It Up"
> "Orange County Girl"

Steps to follow:

1. As you listen to the music, begin moving your body to the beat. Include arm swings, body bends, and jumps.

2. Try to make your dance reflect the meaning of the song. For example, if the music has a happy sound, smile and open your arms.

3. Include a few friends and develop a dance routine.

4. Plan costumes. Choose colors that match the feeling of the dance. Try to create a new look.

5. Perform the dance for your friends and family.

It takes practice to perform dance moves together.

What was it like performing for friends and family? Gwen Stefani performs in front of thousands of people. How do you think that would feel?

Sounds of Music

Like all singers and songwriters, Gwen Stefani has been **influenced** (affected) by different kinds of music. Gwen's parents belonged to a **folk music** group (see box at right). As a child, Gwen enjoyed listening to folk music by singers like Emmylou Harris (see box below) and Bob Dylan.

Folk music

Folk music, also called **traditional music**, comes from the common people of a region. People make up songs and pass them along. Folk music includes work songs and protest songs. The songs are easy to sing. Folk musicians often play guitars and other stringed instruments.

Emmylou Harris

Emmylou Harris was born in Birmingham, Alabama, in 1947. In the 1960s she began singing folk music. She formed a **country music** band in 1973. She is one of the most admired women in country music today.

Emmylou Harris is shown here singing in 2008.

Julie Andrews starred in the 1965 movie *The Sound of Music*.

Musicals

Gwen loves **musicals**. A musical is a play or movie that uses singing and dancing to help tell the story. *Annie* is a musical that Gwen enjoyed as a child (see page 6).

The Sound of Music is Gwen's favorite musical. Even today, if someone asks her, she might sing "I Have Confidence" from *The Sound of Music*. In her 2006 album, *Sweet Escape*, she included a song called "Wind It Up" based on the song "The Lonely Goatherd" from *The Sound of Music*.

Gwen performs "Wind It Up" at a 2006 concert in Los Angeles.

Later influences

In the 1980s Gwen's favorite singer was Sting (see box below). She used to dance to his music. When Gwen began work on her solo albums, she said, "I wanted to recapture the feeling I had when I first heard those songs."

Gwen was also influenced by **rap** music. Rap is a kind of music that features someone speaking to a regular beat. Rap **lyrics** are a kind of poetry. Rap uses rhyme and has a strong beat or rhythm. Gwen's music often includes rap.

Gwen is shown here with Sting in 2003.

Sting

Gordon Matthew Thomas Sumner (known as Sting) was born in Wallsend, England, on October 2, 1951. He is a songwriter, lead singer, and bass player. His band was called The Police. "Every Breath You Take," released in 1983, is one of the band's most famous songs. Sting has sold more than 100 million albums. He has earned 16 Grammy Awards.

Gwen and rapper Eve perform "Rich Girl." This song combines rapping with singing.

Gwen uses **techno music** in her albums, too. Techno is electronic music meant for dancing. It began in Detroit, Michigan, in the 1980s. It uses a machine sound and electronic drums to create a pounding, regular beat. Techno music provides the background for many of Gwen's dance routines.

Combining musical styles

Gwen's songs are considered rock, pop, and dance music. They also sometimes show the influence of songs from musicals. They reflect the many different kinds of music that are important to her. The lyrics are about her life. Gwen says, "I've been a writer from the heart." Her songs talk about love, loneliness, and what it means to be a strong, independent woman.

Another pop icon

Some people compare Gwen Stefani to Madonna (see box below). Both singers are popular, love to dance, and have an individual voice and style. In 2005 Madonna told a reporter that Gwen "ripped me off."

When she heard this, Gwen laughed. She said that every girl her age copied Madonna. Madonna is one of her **idols**. "I always admired her," Gwen said. Madonna may have influenced Gwen, but Gwen's style is her own.

American Idol

In 2007 Gwen appeared on the television singing contest *American Idol* as a special guest. She met with the people competing on the show and offered advice. Then she sang and danced. She was a big hit.

Madonna

Madonna Louise Ciccone (known as Madonna) was born August 16, 1958, in Bay City, Michigan. She moved to New York City to become a dancer. In 1983 she released her first album. She has sold more than 200 million albums worldwide.

Madonna is shown here performing in 2008.

Kid Idol

For this activity, you will organize your own talent show, called *Kid Idol*.

Steps to follow:

1. Gather several friends together. Everyone should choose a song to sing.

2. Use a **karaoke** machine (see box at right). If you do not have one, sing along to your favorite album.

3. Dance or move to the music to make your performance more exciting.

4. Practice together. Can you help one another improve? If Gwen Stefani were watching, what advice do you think she would offer?

5. When everyone is ready, invite family and friends to watch *Kid Idol*. Did you enjoy performing? Would you do it again?

Karaoke

Karaoke is a kind of entertainment that began in Japan in the 1970s. A machine plays the music of a song while a person sings the lyrics into a microphone.

These kids are using a karaoke machine.

Fashion Icon

When Gwen was a child, her mother made many of her clothes. She also made Halloween costumes. Gwen loved dressing up. She enjoyed going to fabric shops with her mother.

Gwen began to make her own clothes when she was in high school. She often bought clothes at secondhand, or thrift stores. She would take the clothes apart and remake them. She even made her own prom dress.

Unusual style

Once she began singing with No Doubt, Gwen designed her own stage clothes. Tony Kanal, a member of No Doubt who was her boyfriend at the time, was Indian. Gwen admired the clothes and jewels that Tony's mother wore. She began copying that style. She wore a stick-on earring in the middle of her forehead as a **bindi**. A bindi is a decoration worn by Indian women.

Gwen's fans wore bindis, too. Gwen wore big, baggy pants, and so did her fans. With her chunky boots, wristbands, and bindi, Gwen created her own special style.

Gwen borrowed ideas from men's fashion to create this outfit for her 2002 No Doubt tour. She added eye-catching extras like the wristbands, belt, and chains.

Hair

In the 1990s Gwen began to dye her brown hair blonde and wear bright-red lipstick. Later she changed her hair color to blue. Then she tried bright pink. By 2000 she again went back to the blonde hair and bright-red lipstick that is her **trademark** (thing she is known for).

In this 1998 photo, blue hair and stick-on decorations give Gwen one-of-a-kind style.

Fashion star

In 2001 Gwen met clothing designer Andrea Lieberman. Andrea helped to design clothing for Gwen's music video "Let Me Blow Ya Mind." Later, Andrea helped Gwen design costumes for her concert tours. Gwen and Andrea enjoyed working together. They joked about creating a clothing line. Then they became serious about it. Gwen started creating her own fashion designs. She named her company L.A.M.B.

L.A.M.B.

In 2003 L.A.M.B.'s first products—bags—went on sale. Clothes soon followed. Gwen hoped to present her fashions at New York Fashion Week. This fashion show is held twice a year. It gives reporters and buyers from clothing stores a chance to see the newest designs. In 2005 models wearing L.A.M.B. clothes appeared at Fashion Week. Songs from *Love.Angel. Music.Baby.* played in the background.

Gwen designed this dress for a 2005 show at New York Fashion Week.

Gwen hired a team to help with the fashion line. By 2008 L.A.M.B. had sold more than $100 million of products. Today, the company sells watches, shoes, bags, and a perfume called L.

L.A.M.B. clothes are expensive. So Gwen created a less costly line of clothing called Harajuku Lovers. This line includes clothes for women, teens, children, and babies.

Lamb

Gwen loves dogs. When she was a child, Gwen had a tiny snow-white dog. She named it Lamb because it followed her everywhere. She named her clothing line after the dog. Then she used the initial letters to name her album *Love.Angel.Music.Baby.*

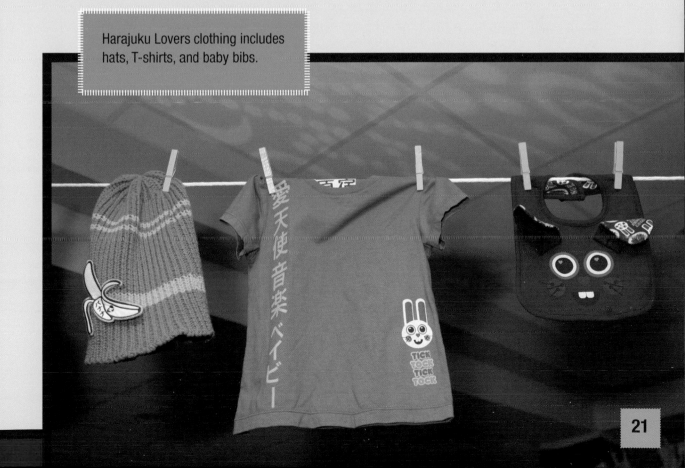

Harajuku Lovers clothing includes hats, T-shirts, and baby bibs.

Show your style

Gwen Stefani has never been afraid to show her style. Fashion experts describe her clothing as hip and edgy. She combines stripes and plaids. She wears tennis shoes with elegant tops, or fancy, spiky heels with T-shirts. Sometimes Gwen chooses flashy jewelry that reflects the light.

Gwen is not afraid to change her style over time, either. She wears what she likes, and people like what she wears.

Now it's your turn to create your own individual style.

Steps to follow:

1. With a friend's help, make a life-size outline of yourself. You can use white paper from a roll or tape several sheets of paper together.

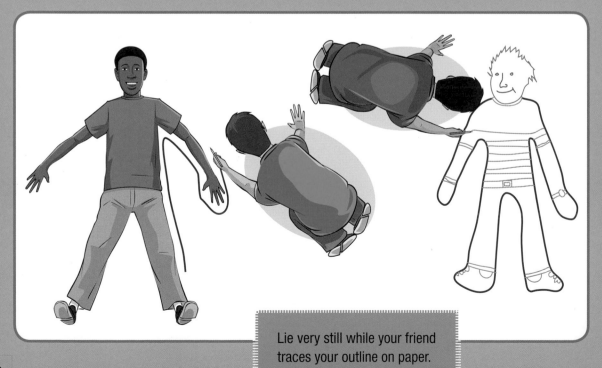

Lie very still while your friend traces your outline on paper.

2. Create an outfit that reflects your style. Will you choose short sleeves or long? Will you wear pants, shorts, or a skirt? Think about accessories—scarves, socks, gloves, ties, belts, and jewelry. Use a pencil to sketch your choices.

3. Use crayons or markers to add colors and designs. Will you choose dark colors or bright ones? Do you prefer plain fabrics, stripes, plaids, or polka dots?

4. Add shoes. Will they be high heels or tennis shoes?

5. Give yourself a special hairstyle.

6. Can you add a musical instrument, book bag, or other details that match your interests?

7. Gwen has sold dolls of herself. She gave each of her dolls a special descriptive name, such as "Tick Tock Gwen," "Cool Gwen," and "Bananas Gwen." Add a descriptive word or words to your own name to make a new name for your creation.

8. Display your new self on a wall or door.

Finishing touches—shoes, hats, sunglasses, headbands, and belts—help to show your style.

Celebrity!

Gwen is pleased when people recognize her. Gwen has met many famous people. She has met Sting and Prince, both **idols** of hers. She was thrilled when Madonna invited her to dinner one night in 2006.

Gwen has traveled the world. She enjoys spending time in Japan. In 1996 she went to the Harajuku section of Tokyo. She visited the shopping district and saw Japanese girls wearing wild clothing. They combined Japanese and Hollywood styles to create a new look. Gwen loved their style.

Fans often recognize Gwen when she goes out. Here she is shown with her husband, Gavin Rossdale.

Gwen was fascinated when she met girls like this one in Tokyo's Harajuku district.

Movie star

In 2004 Gwen played the part of a beautiful movie star in *The Aviator*, starring Leonardo DiCaprio.

The Harajuku girls

Gwen wrote a song called "Harajuku Girls" for *Love.Angel.Music.Baby.* She mentioned them in two other songs. When she went on tour, she took four Harajuku girls as dancers. They followed Gwen everywhere.

Some people thought Gwen was making fun of Japan. The comments surprised Gwen. She says that she included the Harajuku girls to honor their style. "The Harajuku girls is an art project. It's fun," she said.

Malaysian performance

Some people protested when Gwen appeared in Malaysia, in Southeast Asia, in 2007. They felt that her show would be too wild. In Malaysia, performers cannot jump, shout, or toss objects from the stage. Women must be covered from their shoulders to their knees. Gwen respects her audience, so she followed the rules. She wore black tights under her outfits and black gloves up to her elbows. She did not jump, shout, or toss anything from the stage.

Gwen and the Harajuku girls posed for this photo in 2004.

25

Family life

Music and hard work are important to Gwen. So is family. She enjoys spending time with her family.

In 1995 Gwen met Gavin Rossdale, the lead singer and guitar player for the British rock band Bush. They fell in love and later got married on September 14, 2002. Gwen and Gavin live in Los Angeles and in London.

Gwen and Gavin wanted children. On May 26, 2006, their son Kingston James McGregor Rossdale was born. On August 21, 2008, Gwen gave birth to a second son, Zuma Nesta Rock Rossdale.

Gwen took son Kingston and husband Gavin to a New York City fashion show in 2007.

Giving back

Like many stars, Gwen tries to help others. In 2007 she gave money to help people in Orange County, California, who lost their homes to fire. In 2008 she designed a pair of ruby-red slippers like the ones worn by Dorothy in *The Wizard of Oz*. Several shoe designers made red slippers to honor the 1939 movie. The shoes will be sold to help children with the disease **AIDS**.

Staying fresh

While Gwen has been busy being a mom, other singers have stepped up. Nelly Furtado and Fergie (see box below) both released albums in a style similar to Gwen's. Gwen feels honored when someone follows her style. She says that it forces her to move in other directions and to find new music that excites her fans.

Gwen signs autographs for fans in 2006.

Several of Fergie's songs have been hits.

Fergie

Stacy Ferguson (known as Fergie) was born on March 27, 1975, in Hacienda Heights, California. She was a child actor on Nickelodeon's *Kids Incorporated*. She entered the world of music when she joined the **hip-hop** band Black Eyed Peas in 2002.

Timeline

1969	Gwen Stefani is born in Anaheim, California, on October 3.
1986	Gwen joins the band No Doubt.
1987	Gwen graduates from Loara High School in Anaheim. She becomes the lead singer for No Doubt in December. She begins classes at Cypress College in Cypress, California.
1995	No Doubt releases *Tragic Kingdom*.
	Gwen begins dating Gavin Rossdale.
1996	No Doubt begins a world tour.
2000	No Doubt releases *Return of Saturn*.
2001	No Doubt releases *Rock Steady*. Gwen performs with the rapper Eve.
2002	Gwen marries Gavin Rossdale on September 14.
	She wins a Grammy Award for the song "Let Me Blow Ya Mind."

2003	Gwen designs bags for L.A.M.B.
2004	Gwen releases her first solo album, *Love.Angel.Music.Baby.*
2005	Gwen's fashions are shown at New York Fashion Week.
	She wins a Best **Choreography** Grammy Award for "Hollaback Girl."
2006	Gwen releases another solo album, *Sweet Escape*.
	Her son Kingston is born on May 26.
2007	The "Sweet Escape" world tour begins in April.
	Life & Style magazine names Gwen one of "The 10 Most Stylish Stars of 2007."
2008	Gwen's second son, Zuma, is born on August 21.
2009	Gwen and No Doubt go on tour together, after a break of over four years.

Glossary

AIDS short for "acquired immune deficiency syndrome," a disease of the immune system caused by HIV (human immunodeficiency virus). Gwen raised money to help children with AIDS.

bindi small, colored dot worn in the middle of a woman's forehead, common in India. When Gwen wore a bindi, others copied her.

choreography art of creating and arranging dances. Gwen helps plan the choreography of her live shows.

country music simple style of folk music heard mostly in the southern United States. Emmylou Harris sings country music.

digital download content provided over the Internet that can be transferred to another computer. For a fee, people can buy Gwen's songs as digital downloads.

dyslexia learning disorder marked by difficulty recognizing and understanding written words. Gwen has dyslexia.

folk music music created by the common people of a nation or region and spread or passed down by word of mouth. As a child, Gwen listened to folk music.

hip-hop street dancing invented in New York City in the 1970s. Hip-hop dancers toured with Gwen in 2007.

icon someone who is the object of great attention and devotion; an idol. Famous people often become icons.

idol any person or thing who is admired or adored by others. Sting is one of Gwen's idols.

immigrant someone who comes from abroad to live permanently in another country. Immigrants brought ska to Great Britain and the United States.

influence affect a person, thing, or course of events. Madonna influenced Gwen.

jazz kind of music that began in New Orleans, Louisiana, at the beginning of the 1900s. Jazz features trumpets, trombones, clarinets, and saxophones, as well as pianos. Musicians make up variations on the main themes of the music as they play.

karaoke form of entertainment using a machine to play the background music for singing. Karaoke began in Japan.

lyrics words to a song. Gwen writes lyrics that reflect her feelings.

media means of communication such as television, radio, newspapers, and so on. The media report stories about Gwen.

musical play or movie that uses singing and dancing to help tell the story. *Annie* is a musical that Gwen loved as a child.

rap music that features someone speaking to a regular beat. Rap music is very popular today.

ska music that combines African rhythms with Jamaican folk music and U.S. jazz. No Doubt is a ska band.

techno music electronic music with a machine sound and pounding drums. Techno music is a popular kind of dance music.

trademark distinctive mark or feature that is particularly characteristic of or identified with a person or thing. Red lipstick is one of Gwen's trademarks.

traditional music another name for folk music. Gwen grew up listening to traditional music.

Find Out More

Books

Krohn, Katherine. *Gwen Stefani* (*A&E Biography*). Minneapolis: Twenty-First Century, 2007.

Tracy, Kathleen. *Gwen Stefani* (*Blue Banner Biographies*). Hockessin, Del.: Mitchell Lane, 2006.

Websites

Gwen Stefani's official website
www.gwenstefani.com

No Doubt's official website
www.nodoubt.com

The official store of Harajuku Lovers
www.harajukulovers.com

Index

albums 9, 10, 11, 13, 21, 25
  sales 9, 10
American Idol 16
Annie 6, 13
Aviator, The 24
awards 5, 9

bindis 18
Black Eyed Peas 27

CDs 4
celebrity status 5, 24
charity work 26
country music 12

dance routines 10, 11, 15
digital downloads 4
Disney, Walt 7
Disneyland 7
dolls 23
Dylan, Bob 12
dyslexia 7

Eve 15

fashion and style 5, 18–23
Fergie 27
folk music 8, 12
Furtado, Nelly 27

hair style and color 19
Harajuku girls 24, 25
Harajuku Lovers 21
Harris, Emmylou 12
hip-hop 10, 27

icons and idols 5, 16, 24

Japan 6, 17, 24, 25
jazz 8

Kanal, Tony 8, 18
karaoke 17

L.A.M.B. 20–21
Lieberman, Andrea 20
lipstick 19
Love.Angel.Music.Baby 9, 10, 20, 21, 25
lyrics 4, 14, 15

Madness 8
Madonna 16, 24
Malaysia 25
music videos 20
musicals 13

No Doubt 8–9, 10, 18

Prince 24

rap music 14, 15
Return of Saturn 9
Rock Steady 9
Rossdale, Gavin 24, 26

ska 8
songwriting 9, 14, 15
Sound of Music, The 7, 13
Stefani, Gwen
  awards 5, 9
  celebrity status 5, 24
  charity work 26
  clothing lines 20–21
  early life 6–7
  family life 26
  fashion and style 5, 18–22
  film appearance 24
  influences on 12–14
  in No Doubt 8–9
  solo artist 10
  songwriting 9, 14, 15
Sting 14, 24
Sweet Escape 9, 10, 11, 13

talent shows 16, 17
techno music 15
tours 4, 9, 10, 18, 25
Tragic Kingdom 9

Wizard of Oz, The 26